Islām and the Liberation of Slaves

Āyatullāh Nāṣir Makārim Shīrāzī

AL-BURĀQ

Copyright

ISBN: 978-1-956276-46-6
Printed and published by al-Burāq Publications.
Where needed, context and transliterations were added. Some minor edits were made to the translated Arabic text.

Ordering Information
We offer discounts and promotions for wholesale purchases, non-profit organizations, and other educational institutions. Contact us at the email below for further information.

www.al-Buraq.org
publications@al-Buraq.org

First Edition | December 2023

Dedication

The publication of this book was made possible through the generous support of our donors.

Please recite *Sūrat al-Fātihah* and ask God for the Divine reward (*thawāb*) to be conferred upon the donors and also the souls of all the deceased in whose memory their loved ones have contributed graciously towards the publication of *Islām and the Liberation of Slaves*.

We begin by giving all praise and thanks to God ﷻ for giving us the *tawfīq* to translate this book. He has guided us, and without Him, we would not have been guided to the straight path embodied by the Prophet Muḥammad ﷺ and the Ahl al-Bayt ﷿.

This book is dedicated to all the scholars, martyrs, and believers who worked tirelessly to promote the pure Muḥammadan path.

We also want to thank and appreciate all believers worldwide and acknowledge the team that helped al-Burāq Publications complete this work, spending countless hours to make its publication possible. Please recite Sūrat al-Fātiḥah on behalf of them, their families, and their marḥūmīn.

This book is dedicated in honor of the following individuals. Please remember them in your prayers, and may God ﷻ have mercy on them and their loved ones.

Abu Banat	Layth al-Wilzi
AlHassan ElMoussa	Mahmoud Tiba
Ali Deeb Al Haj Hussein	Mehrunisa Ajani
Ali Ftouni	Mohammed Husain Jafri
Ali Hammoud	Munawwar Jehan
Alya Agemy	Rayhana Hammoud
Bande Khuda	Ruqayyah Rasheed
Begum Rizvi	Saina J. Hussain
Fatima S Marashi	Sayyid Sobh H. Sobh
Gulam Ali Aga	Shandar Fatima
Hajj Ahmad Sheet	Siddiqa A. Jafar
Hajj Hassan Sobh	Syed Ali M. Zaidi
Hajj Mohamad Daher	Syed Hassan Jafri
Hajj Sami Ftouni	Syed Jaffer A. Abidi
Hajji Amneh Sobh-Ftouni	Syed Mujtaba Rizvi
Hajji Hiam Hojeije	Syed Nawab R. Kazmi
Hajji Imane Srour	Turfah Sobh
Hasan Zaheer	Yusuf A. Ajani
Imad Khalil	Zahraa Hammoud
Intissar Bazzi	Zainul Abedin Abbas
Kh. Rizvi	Zehra B. Bhojani
Khadijah Rose	Zehra Jaffery

Duʿāʾ al-Ḥujjah

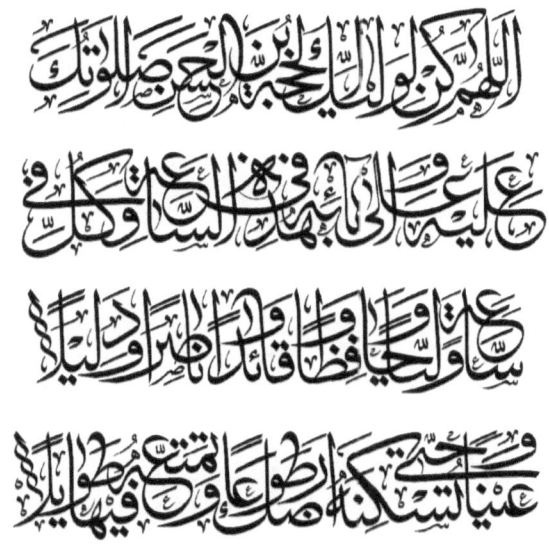

O God, be, for Your representative, the Ḥujjat (proof), son of al-Ḥasan, Your blessings be upon him and his forefathers, in this hour and in every hour: a guardian, a protector, a leader, a helper, a proof, and an eye - until You make him live on the Earth, in obedience (to You), and cause him to live in it for a long time.

Terms of Respect

The following Arabic phrases have been used throughout this book in their respective places to show the reverence the noble personalities deserve.

Used for God, meaning:
Exalted and Sublime (Perfect) is He

Used for Prophet Muḥammad, meaning:
Blessings from God be upon him and his family

Used for a man (singular) of a high status, meaning:
Peace be upon him

Used for a woman (singular) of a high status, meaning:
Peace be upon her

Used for men/women (dual) of high status, meaning:
Peace be upon them both

Used for men and women (plural) of high status, meaning:
Peace be upon them all

Used for Imām Muḥammad al-Mahdī, meaning:
May God hasten his return

Used for a deceased scholar, meaning:
May his resting [burial] place remain pure

Transliteration Table

The method of transliteration of Islāmic terminology from the Arabic language has been carried out according to the standard transliteration table below.

ء	ʾ	ر	r	ف	f
ا	a	ز	z	ق	q
ب	b	س	s	ك	k
ت	t	ش	sh	ل	l
ث	th	ص	ṣ	م	m
ج	j	ض	ḍ	ن	n
ح	ḥ	ط	ṭ	و	w
خ	kh	ظ	ẓ	ه	h
د	d	ع	ʿ	ي	y
ذ	dh	غ	gh		
Long Vowels					
ا	ā	و	ū	ي	ī
Short Vowels					
◌َ	a	◌ُ	u	◌ِ	i

Table of Contents

Preface

In the Name of God, the Beneficent, the Merciful

What will you read in this book?

People often question the benefits offered to humanity by religions (the real ones and not the ones made up). The answer to this question is simple for those familiar with the prophets' stories; however, this small book cannot comprehensively explain the answer. Nonetheless, we have sought to highlight two merits of religion and left the remaining for another book titled "*The Purpose of Sects*".

The two matters this book discusses are as follows:

1. How slaves are liberated under religion

2. The critical role of religions in scientific, cultural, and philosophical movements

We hope this book offers a beneficial and fruitful read for people, particularly the educated youth.

Āyatullāh Nāṣir Makārim Shīrāzī

Islām's Fight Against Slavery

This section will discuss:

- Did Islām endorse slavery?

- Islām's comprehensive plan to liberate slaves.

As is the case, the first people to believe in the Prophet Muḥammad ﷺ were the slaves, and that is because they sought freedom in this new religion and were able to regain their social identity under it.

However, many who are quick to judge from a distance attack Islām in this regard, arguing that if Islām is a divine religion, then why did it endorse slavery and the ensuing issues that arose from it?

As such, materialist Marxists—who claim to be the most concerned with the disenfranchised—focus on this issue and take advantage of it, believing that they could manipulate it into an influential slogan to ultimately confuse the Muslim youths and weaken their religious and Islāmic spirit in this way.

To clarify the weight of these misguided attacks and demonstrate Islām's approach to slavery, it is essential to explore the following subjects:

1. What is meant by the terms slavery and slaves?

2. The historical view regarding slavery (the characteristics of slavery throughout history)

3. Islām's approach to slavery and slaves

4. The final objection

The Definition of Slavery

A slave is a human whose action choices are entirely in the hands of another human, and he is sold and bought similarly to all other belongings. Furthermore, the slave owner exercises the right to do as they please with the slave.

Similar to how people's choices and behavior regarding their properties are influenced by the surrounding environment and the relevant public and private laws, the behavior of slave owners changes and evolves as the times change and the surroundings transform.

Some nations treated slaves with excessive harshness and cruelty, denying them their right to self-defense. For example, some Greeks believed that if they were to attack a slave, the slave had no right to retaliate at all (whether it was against his owner or another person); instead, he had to succumb to the assault.

The Spartans would say that if someone assaulted a slave and cursed at him, then the slave did not have the right to sue him in court! According to Montesquieu, who authored the book *The Spirit of the Laws*, Spartan slaves suffered greatly as every slave belonged to all the members of the society and not just one person, and every person could torture a slave, whether his or someone else's, without fearing the law! As such, it was meaningless to resort to court and sue in a society where killing slaves had no repercussions or conditions and where slaves were treated no differently than animals.

On the other hand, laws that cater to slaves and their interests were rare to find, and one example of these is found in Ancient Rome (according to Montesquieu), where the "master" was obliged to provide food and clothing for his slave as per specific laws. He even had to care for his slave through illness and age.

However, the horrific crimes that were committed against the slaves during the era of slavery around different regions of the world are cause for significant pessimism, making it hard to believe that such laws were sometimes put in place supposedly for the interest of the slaves. However, the truth is that these laws aimed to prolong the slaves' longevity so that they could be taken advantage of to a fuller extent, and even if a law were sympathetic to the slaves, its effect would be negligible in its application.

Ultimately, however, despite all the differences and developments that occurred in the context of the interaction between master and slave over time, the constant across all this is the notion of "exploitation of humans by humans", and that is the core of slavery.

Today, this notion appears in many facets of the current human society. Even if it is not labeled as such, it remains crystal clear that research in this regard revolves around the true essence and practice of slavery, regardless of whether or not it is given this term, as the terminology plays no role in this subject.

The Historical View of Slavery

It is unclear when the era of slavery started in human history, meaning that if we were to go back to the most distant ages, we would find different forms of slavery permeating human societies. However, the main driving factor of slavery involves defeat in battle and war prisoners—which is the most viable possibility. For this reason, some researchers traced the history of slavery to the start of wars between people. On the other hand, this author believes that if we were to investigate this issue more broadly, we would find that the main contributing factor is the coinciding presence of weak individuals and influential individuals with a streak of control and exploitation at the same time. This phenomenon was largely present between the members of the same tribe until before tribal wars. Furthermore, scholars in law reinforce this notion as they highlight another fundamental factor of slavery: indebted people who suffer from poverty resort to selling themselves to their lenders (this law was particularly prevalent) under the pressure of the lenders' demands. As such, we cannot confine the history of slavery to the history of wars in human society.

Slavery remained prevalent up until the middle of the nineteenth century (around 130 years), and the movement to abolish slavery began worldwide after this period. In this regard, Britain was perhaps the forerunner as after only a short period (in 1840), the practice of auctioning slaves was abolished even in the colonies! Moreover, slavery was prevalent in France up until the French Revolution of 1848, and it persisted in the Netherlands until 1863, after which the practice of selling and buying slaves was banned.

Similarly, slavery was widespread in America up until 1860; however, after this year, North America and South America engaged in deadly battles (i.e., the American Civil War) in this regard. The Southerners were firmly in favor of slavery due to their pressing need for slaves in the farms, leading to the conflict with the Northerners, who largely lacked a need for slaves. These clashes persisted for four years and were also known as the "War of Separation" [among other names]. The war ended in favor of the northerners, thus abolishing slavery throughout America. In the late nineteenth century (around ninety years), all countries agreed to ban slavery, and ever since then, any practices of selling and buying slaves were undertaken away from the public.

Nonetheless, it is imperative to highlight that the development of machines and new techniques, societies growing closer, and the discovery of new energies that largely replaced slaves significantly contributed to the abolishment of slavery.

The Changing Forms of Slavery

At the same time, it is not accurate that slavery was abolished entirely from this era; rather, slavery and the exploitation of humans—unfortunately—returned in a more dangerous and horrifying form: the enslavement of colonies and nations, which is termed as "colonialism". Although colonialism is traced back to times before the abolishment of slavery, we can say that while slavery on the level of individuals was weakening and decaying, mass slavery and colonialism were beginning to take root and becoming increasingly vital. Unfortunately, the calamities brought upon by the slavery of individuals re-emerged in a more horrific form during the era of colonialism!

During this period, the abhorrent term "slavery" was replaced with the more appealing term "colonialism", which means—in fact—"striving on the path of reconstruction" (on the surface, it connotes the reconstruction of weak states, but on a deeper and more obscure level, it means expanding and growing the colonizers' kingdoms). However, shortly after, the truth behind colonialism was revealed; to illustrate this, we read in the "*al-Mukhtar*" dictionary the following:

"The term colonialism—currently—means the aggressive intervention of a powerful country in a weak country, extorting its money and abusing its will and rights; furthermore, colonial countries are known as powerful countries that assume control of weak nations under the guise of reconstructing them!"

Here, it is noteworthy that the forerunners in abolishing slavery (such as Britain) were also among the first to colonize inhabited territories with bountiful resources, including the Indian region under British control. Thus, great working nations who sought to meet their basic needs were forced to succumb to colonial slavery!

The relationships between the powerful countries and the colonies were among history's most oppressive and horrific accounts. Discussing the heinous crimes of colonialism (which are still largely ongoing in some regions) could be uncomfortable for both the speaker and listener; nonetheless, allow me—dear reader— to highlight an example and a fraction of what has garnered the attention of people today (this part was taken from the draft of the book *Revelation or Symbolic Feeling*).

Primarily, it is essential to listen to the claims of orientalists themselves to understand how these civilized countries treated colonies from their perspective.

In his book *The History of Civilization*, Dr. Gustave Le Bon says the following regarding the colonial situation in the Indian region:

"While it is true that London flourished with wealth and thrived, the people whose resources were stolen descended into the worst levels of poverty and destitution." He continues (observing closely), "According to official counts, there are 16,000,000 beggars today in the state of 'Madras'. That is only natural as the impoverished inhabitants have to pay 400,000,000 pounds in fees to the Ministry of War. They also have to cover fees of 50,000,000 pounds for all the other state departments and send a total of 500,000,000 pounds exclusively to the British Treasury after all these expenses!...

When the requirement of this 500,000,000 pounds fee was announced, the British retorted with a vehement reply in a well-known newspaper: this amount covers the expenses of the administration and the secure and organized government founded for the Indians!"

However, this fails to recognize that the annual damages in terms of hunger and poverty incurred by this "secure and organized" administration far exceeded the losses of a grisly war—without exaggeration!

Moreover, Grandidier says, "The class of farmers and agriculture workers constituted the majority, and they used to pay a sixth of their profits in taxes when the feudal lords governed them. When the British came, they had to pay half their profits (meaning 3/6), and if anyone evaded paying these taxes, their properties would be seized." He adds, "In this way, farmers were forced into an unimaginably perishable state!"

Furthermore, after extensive research on the form and role of the British government in India, the British Hindman clarifies that "the British put the people under the heavy pressure of taxes that starve them from one side and break the industry on the other, forcing factories to close in order to increase imports." Then, he makes a pleasant prediction,

"We are walking the path towards an extraordinary disaster and tragedy in history!"... In truth, what is a greater tragedy for Britain than the Indians demanding independence and chasing this empire out of India?

In another instance, the British man says, "Among the most horrific issues is that the north-western states were forced to export their agricultural products abroad when, in the meantime, 300,000 of the inhabitants perished of starvation in a few months."

In 1887, according to official statistics, only 935,000 inhabitants from the state of "Madras" perished. It is noteworthy that Hindman had published these statistics in a well-known newspaper at the time without making any criticism!

Does this not constitute mass slavery? Did they do any worse during the dark era of slavery?

Ultimately, it is enlightening to consider their own opinions on these two eras, as the orientalist above frankly expresses in one of his speeches, "The British treatment of the Indians is a thousand times worse than the treatment of the slaves!"

Another dark account of mass slavery and colonialism, which the Orientalist Europeans considered the most tragic page of their history, is the way Europeans handled China. In this regard, after discussing the heinous crimes of the colonizers in China, one such orientalist says, "One day, perhaps, our future generations will be gravely punished for our terrible actions, and the Chinese will exact revenge on them!"

In reality, this prediction later came true as the great country of China joined the ranks of the countries that opposed these usurpers and aggressors after the Communist movement and coup occurred.

Furthermore, another similar account of history involves the relationship between the "civilized" countries and the rural masses in America and Oceania after its discovery. In this regard, it is sufficient to refer to what Gustave Le Bon writes, "To the civilized people of Europe, the beasts (ruralists) of America and Oceania are like the rabbit to the hunter!... As we see today, all of them have gone unheeded."

On the other hand, the approach that France—the supposed leader of freedom and civilization and the opposer of liberation movements—adopted in its treatment of its colonies in North Africa, particularly with the Muslim population in Algeria, is a prime example of slavery and cruelty that does not need further clarification. Even worse than all this is the silence of the "civilized" world in the face of these crimes under the pretext that "the issues of Algeria are considered an internal situation for France."

Another horrific account of mass slavery is the "red slavery," whose ill-fated and terrible effects fell on Eastern Europe.

Although communists considered themselves the sole advocates of human rights and freedom from the chains of slavery, they have perhaps freed a man from one chain but then shackled him with a more powerful one!

Regardless of the political media that promote or oppose communism, there is much evidence of the people's lack of freedom in the communist states, particularly communist states located in Eastern Europe, as they—in fact—suffered a form of imprisonment and were indeed not free to self-determine. Suppose we were to lend truth to the horrific accounts of what went on in the forced labor camps in Russia, combined with the brutal and large-scale executions that would occur in short periods in their regime apparatus. In that case, we can only call this social system "mass slavery"!

Undoubtedly, some believe that the era of colonialism, too, has been decaying and coming to an end and that the colonies have started seeking their independence one by one, feeling confident that colonialism in all its forms (black and red) and impacts will someday be completely eradicated. However, the transformations and changes in the current situation are shallow and superficial at best. The core of slavery is ever-present in new forms, and the only difference is in its name and terminology. As long as the concept of "the powerful and the weak" persists and the teachings of faith and morals do not take root in this world, then this situation will never change, and the notion of "the exploitation of humans by humans" will keep resurfacing, disguised in new forms every day!

Islām's Approach Toward Slaves

Islām came to a society where slaves were living under excruciating conditions. At the time, society did not even allow women the right to life - as the practice of female infanticide was most prevalent. Hence, it is relatively straightforward how such a society would treat slaves whom they do not even consider human.

As such, Islām began affecting broad reforms related to the issue of slaves, which did not have any advocates at the time. These large-scale reforms were part of Islām's comprehensive and radical reforms regarding all human life affairs.

Islām's reform plan for slaves includes many articles, the most important of which are generally as follows:

Article 1: To improve the conditions of the slaves, Islām first recognized that they were part of human society, thus expanding the circle of religious duties and teachings to include the slaves equally as everyone else. Islām eliminated all prevalent prerogatives and established piety and virtues as indicators of merit; in this regard, God ﷻ says,

﴿يَٰٓأَيُّهَا ٱلنَّاسُ إِنَّا خَلَقْنَٰكُم مِّن ذَكَرٍ وَأُنثَىٰ وَجَعَلْنَٰكُمْ شُعُوبًا وَقَبَآئِلَ لِتَعَارَفُوٓا۟ إِنَّ أَكْرَمَكُمْ عِندَ ٱللَّهِ أَتْقَىٰكُمْ إِنَّ ٱللَّهَ عَلِيمٌ خَبِيرٌ﴾

⟨yā-'ayyuhā n-nāsu 'innā khalaqnākum min dhakarin wa-'unthā wa-ja'alnākum shu'ūban wa-qabā'ila li-ta'ārafū 'inna 'akramakum 'inda llāhi 'atqākum 'inna llāha 'alīmun khabīr^{un}⟩

⟨O mankind! Indeed, We created you from a male and a female, and made you nations and tribes that you may identify yourselves with one another. Indeed the noblest of you in the sight of God is the most Godwary among you. Indeed God is Knowing, Aware⟩[1]

Moreover, Islām granted slaves the right to complain and plead in court, similar to everyone else.

Article 2: Islām issued numerous orders that mandate treating slaves humanely and kindly and engaging with them courteously to the extent that they became partners and contributors in their masters' lives and livelihoods.

In this regard, the Prophet Muḥammad ﷺ says,

> "If someone has his brother under his authority, he should feed him from what he

---

[1] Sūrat al-Ḥujurāt, Verse 13

eats, clothe him from what he wears, and not burden him with anything that will be too much for him. If you burden him with what will be too much for him, then help him."[2]

It was reported that Imām 'Alī b. Abī Ṭālib ﷺ told his servant Qanbar,

"I feel embarrassed, in front of my Lord, to be kind to you; for I heard the Messenger of God say,

"Clothe them from what you wear and feed them from what you eat."[3]

Furthermore, it was also reported that Imām Ja'far al-Ṣādiq ﷺ said that if he gave his servant an order and noticed that it was extraneous, then he would personally help him with it.[4] Suffice it to say that

---

[2] al-Hindī, 'Alī al-Muttaqī, *Kanz al-'Ummāl fī Sunan al-Aqwāl wal-Af'āl*, Vol. 9, p. 2, number 35009.

[3] al-Ḥakim al-Nīshābūrī, *al-Mustadrak 'ala al-Ṣaḥīḥayn,,* Vol. 3, p. 39, chapter 13.

[4] Majlisī, 'Allamah Muḥammad Bāqir, *Biḥār al-Anwār,* Vol. 15, p. 41.

there are numerous other examples of such narrations.

Article 3: Islām organized a comprehensive plan for the liberation and emancipation of slaves, aiming to enable them to enjoy the blessing of freedom over a short and gradual period (without incurring adverse reactions).

On the one hand, Islām remarkably recommended the liberation and manumission of slaves; as the Prophet Muḥammad ﷺ says,

> "He who frees another Muslim, God delivers every one of his organs from Hellfire."

This narration is reported repeatedly in multiple wordings.

According to existing evidence, the Prophet Muḥammad ﷺ considered that keeping a slave and refraining from freeing him is an abhorrent action. Furthermore, whenever one of his servants committed a righteous deed, he would say,

"Go, you are free. I hate to use a man who belongs with the people of Paradise."[5]

In the book *al-Wasā'il*, one chapter provides insightful accounts and narrations that ultimately report that a slave is automatically liberated after seven years of servitude, regardless of whether his master approves or not.[6]

In addition to all the previous, prominent religious figures used to lead by example and encourage people to set the slaves free. For instance, it is reported that Imām 'Alī b. Abī Ṭālib ﷺ, the Commander of the Faithful, had set free thousands of slaves alone![7]

Under this goal, Islām put in place rules and regulations that mandated the freedom of the slave despite the owner's objections. For instance, Islāmic jurisprudence describes two forms of conditional manumission: "tadbīr" and

---

[5] al-Ḥurr al-'Āmilī, Shaykh Muḥammad b. al-Ḥasan, *Wasā'il al-Shī'a*, *The Book of Manumission*, ch. 1.

[6] al-Ḥurr al-'Āmilī, Shaykh Muḥammad b. al-Ḥasan, *Wasā'il al-Shī'a*, *The Book of Manumission*, ch. 8 and 20.

[7] *al-Jawāher al-Nafīs*, the chapter on manumission, Vol. 5.

"mukātabah", each of which has detailed provisions.

Tadbīr is the manumission of a slave upon the death of his master; as such, a slave is set free in the case that his master passes away. Mukātabah involves the manumission of a slave on the condition that he pays a certain amount of money (which is typically less than or equal to the slave's value). If the slave cannot do so, then the Sharīʿa ruler must cover it from the treasury using the shares of alms money (*zakāt*).

All these regulations are evidence of the significant consideration that Islām dedicated to the matter of the slaves' liberation.

On the other hand, in jurisprudence books[8], we read of many means upon which a slave is automatically or by the master's compulsion set free:

First, Automatic freedom entails that a slave can liberate himself by himself through the following means:

---

[8] al-Ḥurr al-ʿĀmilī, Shaykh Muḥammad b. al-Ḥasan, *Wasāʾil al-Shīʿa*, Vol. 16, p. 36, chapter 36 — manumision.

1. If the master manumits a part of his slave, it also applies to the rest of him, and the slave is thus wholly free. This is an indicator of Islām's desire to free slaves for the most minor or most superficial of reasons.

2. If he becomes the owner of his father, mother, grandparents, children, uncle, aunt, brother, and sister, they are set free automatically.

3. If a slave loses his sight or becomes a frail elderly man, then the right to ownership is taken away from his master, and the treasury covers the needs of the freed slave.

4. A slave is set free if he reverts to Islām before his master in wartime.

5. A slave is immediately freed if his master cuts his ear or nose off.

6. If the master fathers children from his concubine, he cannot sell her in the future and must keep and care for her until she is freed from the share of her children's inheritance. Naturally, this is a means to liberate a significant number of slaves.

7. If one of the parents is free and the other a slave, then their offspring is free.

Second: Mandatory or compulsory liberation is required in many cases where a Muslim is obligated to manumit a slave under the requirements of a vow or as expiation for fasting or an act of killing.

Ultimately, by implementing this large-scale and comprehensive plan and the significant consideration given to this issue, Islām set the stage for the gradual liberation and emancipation of slaves, thus ensuring that the next generation and their offspring are granted freedom rightfully.

Some might wonder: why didn't Islām give a final and comprehensive order to liberate all slaves? This kind of thinking is irrational immature, and stems from inexperience in social matters. If we consider the high prevalence of slavery at the time and the fact that most people dealt with selling and buying slaves, then we would conclude that such an abrupt decision would end up in sky-high unemployment and homelessness rates, and that is not a viable situation.

The surprising aspect after these long centuries is that the abolishment of slavery in America came at the cost of a grisly war that lasted four years and left behind many casualties. Given this, how can we believe that no severe reaction would have ensued if Islām had abolished slavery all at once during that turbulent dark age?

Hence, if we look closely, we will find that Islām's approach to the liberation of slaves is a precise, rational, and effective one that is safeguarded from all potential types of reactions.

The Implications of this Cause from Others' Perspectives

Here, it is appropriate to quote what the famous Christian historian Jurjī Zaydān expressed[9] in this regard:

"Islām came as a mercy to the slaves, and so, the Prophet ﷺ commended treating them well, saying 'do not burden the slaves with that which they cannot bear and feed them from what you eat' and 'do not call them your bondman and slave-girl; rather, say my boy and my girl'. As the Noble Qur'ān says,

---

[9] Zaydān, Jurjī, *Tārīkh al-Tamaddun al-Islāmī*, Vol. 2, p. 327.

﴿وَٱعْبُدُوا۟ ٱللَّهَ وَلَا تُشْرِكُوا۟ بِهِۦ شَيْـًٔا وَبِٱلْوَٰلِدَيْنِ إِحْسَٰنًا وَبِذِي ٱلْقُرْبَىٰ وَٱلْيَتَٰمَىٰ وَٱلْمَسَٰكِينِ وَٱلْجَارِ ذِي ٱلْقُرْبَىٰ وَٱلْجَارِ ٱلْجُنُبِ وَٱلصَّاحِبِ بِٱلْجَنۢبِ وَٱبْنِ ٱلسَّبِيلِ وَمَا مَلَكَتْ أَيْمَٰنُكُمْ إِنَّ ٱللَّهَ لَا يُحِبُّ مَن كَانَ مُخْتَالًا فَخُورًا﴾

﴿wa-ʿbudū llāha wa-lā tushriku bihī shayʾan wa-bi-l-wālidayni ʾiḥsānan wa-bi-dhī l-qurbā wa-l-yatāmā wa-l-masākīni wa-l-jāri dhī l-qurbā wa-l-jāri l-junubi wa-ṣ-ṣāḥibi bi-l-janbi wa-bni s-sabīli wa-mā malakat ʾaymānukum ʾinna llāha lā yuḥibbu man kāna mukhtālan fakhūra﴾

﴿Worship God and do not ascribe any partners to Him, and be good to parents, the relatives, the orphans, the needy, the near neighbour and the distant neighbour, the companion at your side, the traveller, and your slaves. Indeed God does not like those who are arrogant and boastful﴾[10]

The Origins of Slavery

The final argument that could be raised against Islām is as follows: while it is true that Islām organized a full-fledged plan to liberate the slaves,

---

[10] Sūrat al-Nisāʾ, Verse 36.

why did it give people a means to enslave others and allow the practice of selling and buying war prisoners as slaves?

This is the last claim that could be made in this regard, and it is easily refutable if we were not quick to pass judgment and instead conducted a careful analysis of this issue.

Undoubtedly, civilized countries and their partisans cannot invoke such an argument. That is because of the way these countries treated war prisoners—upon achieving victory in war—and the accounts of released prisoners reveal that they had practiced one of the worst forms of slavery, even if it was not called so. The countries that emerged victorious from World War II treated the defeated ten times worse than slaves would have been!

In this context, it is necessary to highlight two issues:

First, To understand the situation of war prisoners, we must take note of the opposing party that is fighting against Islām and the rulings of jihād in Islām. In brief, jihād in Islām is against that which does not align with the rulings of God, truth, and justice and does not yield to proper logic. That is because Islām clearly does not fight anyone for political aims or financial interests; national and geographic differences and the clash in the interests of nations are certainly not cause for war. In truth, jihād in Islām is the struggle between truth and falsehood and between justice and oppression on the path to liberate mankind.

If the rulings of jihād were applied accurately, then there would be no one left in the opposing party except for those who firmly deny the truth and consider that implementing the just Islāmic rulings would go against their interests. So, such people only contribute to disrupting society and misguide the people.

However, in brief, even if these rulings were not executed correctly during the reign of some Caliphs (i.e., rulers) and some individuals were, as a result, enslaved unjustly, then Islām cannot be made the culprit behind this because our research is related to the laws of Islām and their social consequences.

Second, Contrary to what some think, the enslavement of war prisoners is not a mandatory ruling; instead, Muslims must bring the prisoners to the Sharī'a ruler or the leader of the Muslims after the war is over—noting that no one has the right to kill them. Considering the interests of the Muslims in terms of time and place, the leader resorts to one of the following three actions:

1. Issue an order of their release with no conditions or restrictions

2. Issue an order of their release in return for payment, as deemed necessary

3. Issue an order of their enslavement, taking them as slaves if the need to do so arises

As such, the ruling of enslavement is not mandatory and is, instead, flexible, and it can also be foregone if need be.[11]

According to Muslim thinkers, the Islāmic government is tasked with choosing from these three actions in a way that preserves the Muslims' best interests. For example, suppose the circumstances at some point necessitated the enslavement of war prisoners, meaning that the prisoners could not be apprehended or reformed in

---

[11] Refer to the book *Masālik al-Afhām*, Vol. 1, *Book of Jihād*, the section on war prisoners.

any other way, and there was currently no prison or a temporary detention center to maintain them. In that case, this ruling can be applied. However, if we considered the temporal and spatial circumstances and did not feel the need for this ruling, and if we felt that it could cause harm in our current age, then it is essential to dismiss this ruling and elect, instead, the most suitable ruling from among the other two. Ultimately, taking into account the above, no debate remains regarding the issue of war prisoners.

Islām's Program Regarding Slaves

So, what is Islām's approach regarding slaves? Did it endorse or reject slavery? Is Islām an advocate of slaves' freedom, or did it allow the exploitation of humans by humans? In truth, Islām's approach in this regard is crystal clear and impeccable. It is based on granting freedom gradually by establishing a program through which slaves are gradually liberated and integrated into society. For this transitional stage (the transition of slaves into the broad social circle), there is also a dedicated approach through which slavery is abolished in its previous form.

To explain this approach, one must focus attention on three matters:

Freedom is a Fundamental Pillar

Through the Noble Qur'ān, which represents the primary law of Islām, it is clear that Islām invested large-scale efforts to liberate man in all domains, including, for example, liberating man's mind from superstitions such as worshiping idols and other delusions, freeing man from national and tribal prejudices, and liberating man from mass slavery as was the case in the government of the Nimrods, Pharaohs, and their likes. Accordingly, we observe today that owing to Islām's extensive efforts, colonized nations resort to Islām's rulings and instructions to achieve freedom.

For instance, Black Americans have demonstrated a high rate of conversion into Islām, and Islām's rulings have become widespread among the members of this class whose legitimate rights were constantly violated under large global organizations. Furthermore, many colonized African countries turned to Islām, including some of the presidents in these nations; for example, the president of Gabon reverted to Islām and announced to the media that the reason why he leans towards Islām is its liberating spirit and its fight against national prejudices. Similarly, Islām's slogans in liberation movements, such as the Algerian liberation movement, are prime examples of this truth.

Therefore, it is not possible to claim that Islām endorses the notion of "exploitation of humans by humans" or that it chose to remain silent in the face of this issue and did not fight to abolish slavery. In this regard, a well-known hadith among the Imāms of the Muslims is clear proof of what we argued: "The worst of people are those who sell people." Accordingly, the worst type of people are those who seek to enslave others, and Islām's view of man's freedom is based on this concept.

Freedom without a Reaction

Some might question, "If so, then why didn't Islām announce full-fledged freedom on a certain day and time? Why did the gradual emancipation of slaves become the main principle of Islām's approach to the liberation of slaves?" Ultimately, those familiar with the high sensitivity of social issues can understand the philosophy behind the Islāmic rules.

For example, nations often expel the citizens of another nation due to their differences on some issues, and if their number is small, then it matters little. However, if the number of citizens is among tens or hundreds of thousands, then this act would create a significant social issue for the country of these expelled citizens who came back there. That is because these swathes of people will be unemployed, and if they cannot join society, many issues and troubles are bound to occur in terms of the risk to their lives and the risk that society cannot absorb.

Therefore, if the Prophet ﷺ had ordered the emancipation of all slaves on a particular day and time, then tens or hundreds of thousands would be without work or shelter or refuge in the current [of that specific day] society that does not yet have the capacity and capability to absorb all these freed slaves in one day. This would undoubtedly pose a dangerous social issue for the slaves who will perish and the society where they will remain lost and confused.

In light of this, and accordance with the Divine order, Islām implemented a gradual approach toward the liberation of slaves and their integration into society so that they do not become a cancerous tumor that endangers them in the foremost. For this reason, Islām first sought to eliminate the origins of slavery and cut off its roots, except for the issue of the war prisoners that could not be resolved in any other way at the time (the prisons were not capable of accepting the war prisoners at the time), and even in this matter, the Islāmic Government was flexible, providing the choice to either enslave them, take payment in return to their freedom, or liberate them (all as deemed necessary).

Ultimately, Islām utilized all possible means to emancipate slaves by stigmatizing the practice of selling slaves as an ugly and objectionable act, making the act of manumitting a slave a means of expiation of many sins, and establishing just methods for their liberation such as tadbeer and mukataba (which were previously explained). Finally, Islām considered the act of freeing slaves a great act of worship and a recommended act. In this way, Islām paved the way toward gradual freedom.

Elevating the Slaves' Status

Undoubtedly, Islām's approach towards gradual freedom for slaves encompasses a transitional stage during which the slaves are prepared to shift from the past situation and integrate into the free society. As such, Islām considered this matter and thus invested extensive efforts to minimize the slaves' suffering, elevate their status, and ensure their well-being.

In this stage, Islām abolished the former understanding of slavery in which the slave is powerless and akin to a weak animal; instead, he became a proper worker or employee—even an associate and colleague to his master at times.

In the biography of Imām 'Alī b. Abī Ṭālib ﷺ, we read that the Imām once bought two robes, one costing three silver coins and the other costing two silver coins, and he then ordered his boy whom he freed, "Qanbar", to take the former while he kept the latter for himself.[12]

Similarly, we read in the biography of Imām 'Alī al-Riḍā ﷺ that when food is served, he would not eat until all his workers and boys came. Furthermore, the Prophet Muḥammad's mu'adhin [a man who calls Muslims for prayer] and spokesman was his servant, Bilāl al-Ḥabashī, whom he set free.

---

[12] The Twelve Imāms / Hashem Maaruf al-Husseini, Vol. 1, p. 305.

On this point, a question comes to mind: in our present world, is any leader or president equal to his workers and servants regarding clothing, food, and all other facets of life? Moreover, was slavery in its previous [severe and oppressive] form during the transitional stage? Or weren't the slaves' conditions substantially improved and better than the conditions of workers in advanced industrial countries today?

All set forth herein clarifies Islām's humane approach in this domain.

Islām and Scientific Progress

The Great Gift

This brief and concise research aims to provide insight into the answer to the following questions: What great gift did religion offer as a divine message to man? What are the achievements that this message made? What are the changes that could occur in man's society and mind? Before answering these questions, providing a simple definition of religion is essential.

If we were to define religion easily, then we would briefly say the following: "Religion is the collection of beliefs, notions, rulings, customs and norms (i.e., Sunan) through which man reaches human perfection, his soul is complemented, his life is built on happiness and peace, and he prepares himself for a loftier life in the Hereafter." Ultimately, these beliefs and those laws, morals, ethics, and norms all collectively form the basis for religion.

Furthermore, scholars of faith and ideology have clarified the concept of religion in three short phrases, saying that religion is compliance and acceptance through "belief in the heart, endorsement in speech, and practical actions."[13] These three elements are collectively termed religion.

In this regard, the Arabic word "al-Janān" means heart, while "al-Jinān" (notice the different vowels) is the plural of "Jannah", meaning garden or orchard. These words indeed stem from one common origin; "al-Jinān", "al-Jinn", "al-Jannah", and "al-Jonon" - all related semantically to the concept of concealment and occultation.

In this sense, the fetus is called "Janīn" in Arabic because it is hidden away in the uterus, and the garden is called "Jannah" because its earth is hidden under the trees. An insane person is called "Majnūn" in Arabic because his mind has been concealed behind a veil. Similarly, the heart is named "Jinān" because it is hidden in man's chest, and "Jinn" is a creation that cannot be seen because it is hidden from sight.

If we were to delve further into this topic to provide a fuller explanation of the concept of

---

[13] al-Ḥakim al-Nīshābūrī, *al-Mustadrak ʿala al-Ṣaḥīḥayn*, Vol. 2, p. 271.

religion, we would conclude that the truth of religion is the absolute submission to God ﷻ.

Ultimately, religion is the absolute submission to God ﷻ and His will. In other words, the true meaning of religion is for man to submit to the reality and truths of the mortal world, thus enabling him to reach true religion and faith.

Please pay close attention to the following as I would like to clarify this notion in more detail further:

Religion is the submission of man's soul and body to the reality and truths of the world, and to justify this interpretation of religion, we must refer to the roots of this subject as follows:

The Divine laws of the religions that the prophets delivered from God ﷻ for the people and that became whole over time are—in fact—complementary to the laws of creation. The religious rulings and teachings are not separate from the mortal world, and all creations in this world grow and develop via the laws of the prophets of God ﷻ. Through their teachings, approaches, and efforts, the prophets sought to help mankind reach the ultimate goal outlined in the laws of the mortal world.

Allow me, dear reader, to illustrate this idea with a simple example in this regard:

Man is one of the truths of the mortal world, and he was created with a group of spiritual and physical instincts, biases, and impulses specific to him. One of these instincts is the sexual instinct; God ﷻ planted this impulse in humans and animals to ensure the continuity of their progeny [through reproduction]. Accordingly, what is the view of religion on this sexual instinct? Can religion fight to suppress the sexual instinct? Today, this is the case for the Christian Church and priests who believe that it is of utmost necessity to combat the sexual instinct and that it not only is an omen of the devil but also represents the devil inside man!

As such, Catholic priests abstain from marriage and practically seek to suppress this impulse, claiming that the priest cannot fully achieve priesthood if he does not abandon his sexual urges!

Hence, the question remains: can religion impose this? Of course not, and that is because religious teachings came to complement the laws of instinct and the way that man was created. Any system that fights to eradicate human instincts is indeed a man-made concept and not a divine law. The religious system and its different parts do not allow for contrast and contradiction.

Just as the creation belongs to God ☙, so does religion, and both systems related to God ☙ shall never contrast each other. That is why Islām did not order the complete suppression of the sexual instinct; instead, it considers the law that governs sexual matters and the sexual impulse to be among the universal norms in the life of man. In this regard, the Prophet ☙ said,

> "Marriage is part of my sunnah, and whoever does not follow my sunnah has nothing to do with me."[14]

However, Islām prevents this instinct from deviating, overtaking man, and becoming corrupt. Ultimately, Islām works on shaping and guiding it appropriately to reach the pursuant goal.

---

[14] al-Sabziwārī, *Jāmiʿ al-Aḥkām al-Sharʿiyyah*.

Hence, all religious laws must be congruent with this ultimate goal, guiding and shaping feelings, emotions, instincts, and everything related to human existence and creation. As such, we will observe that these two systems complement each other perfectly in all other domains.

Accordingly, the religious laws came to complete the development system of man's existence; in other words, they were set forth to guide mankind to the final stages of perfection on the path toward happiness. Thus, the religious and divine laws complement man's soul, body, and all other laws of existence.

To have faith in religious laws and practices means to believe in the natural laws that govern creation, and this faith is, in effect, man submitting to these realistic truths of the world of existence and design.

However, it is noteworthy here that submitting to the truths of existence implies believing in and acknowledging them; conversely, "ideology" involves submitting to these truths from the inner depths of the heart, mind, and soul and acting upon them.

Amongst the truths of existence is the principle of creation. Submitting to this truth means believing, from the heart and soul, in the presence of God 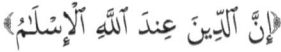. Faith in God 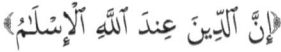 means to endorse and submit to one truth in the world of existence and creation; as the laws and teachings set forth by the prophets and messengers complement the laws of creation, then having faith in them means believing in the laws of the world of existence.

On this basis, the following statement: religion is the submission of man's body and soul to the truths of the world of existence and creation. This, in return, dramatically clarifies the relationship between religion and science. The core and spirit of religion lie in this statement as well. Similarly, and astonishingly, the Noble Qurʾān—our great Divine book that established the supreme sciences for mankind—interprets religion again and says,

﴿إِنَّ ٱلدِّينَ عِندَ ٱللَّهِ ٱلۡإِسۡلَٰمُ﴾

﴿*inna d-dīna ʿinda llāhi l-ʾislāmu*﴾

﴿*Indeed, with God religion is Islām*﴾[15]

---

15 Sūrat Āl ʿImrān, Verse 19.

45

Islām means the "submission" of the mind, body, and soul in front of God ﷻ and His Will and the truths of creation and existence towards justice and truth.

Submitting to anything requires believing in it. Hence, the submission of man's soul is adopting belief in it; the submission of man's body means acting by its rulings and laws; the submission by tongue means endorsing and acknowledging it in speech. Ultimately, all these ideas are included in the statement above.

As such, we have completed our research in this regard in a very brief and concise manner, and we have concluded that the truth of religion is the endorsement of and submission to the sacred Divine, the Divine rulings, and the laws of the world of existence and creation, implementing these laws and benefiting from these capacities logically and adequately.

Religion Throughout Human History

One may wonder: did religion have a special standing over the different ages of mankind? In more precise terms, throughout human history and prehistoric times, is there any age during which man was present, but religion was not? Can we believe those who claim today that we did not choose a religion for ourselves, and is it true that they do not have a religion? Or has religion always been present and will remain as such since man was created?

In all honesty, one cannot think of the nature of man without thinking of religion; man cannot bear an ideological void, and that is why, if we were to examine the different ages of human history closely, we would not find a single period during which man lived without an ideology. Why? Because man is part of this universal system and is closely linked to it, man is connected to this system not only in terms of his body and soul but also on the level of ideology and religion. Therefore, we cannot perceive any age of man to be void of religion.

Let us first go back to [recorded] human history and ask: when did this history begin?

Historians and sociologists say that human history was recorded six thousand years ago in Egypt and then in Chaldea and Assyria. Primarily, human history is traced back to the times when writing first started or the age when civil life came to be after despicable and chaotic times. If we were to calculate the time intervals for both these cases, we would find that around six thousand years have passed in human history. Afterward, it is essential to investigate all the historical records that were proven credible during these six thousand years, including the non-Islāmic records.

For instance, in the historical records by Albert Malet, who briefly mentioned this period, the impact of religion is deeply rooted in all human societies since the very first moments of [recorded] human history. The history of the Egyptians, as the first of human cultures worldwide, and then that of the Chaldeans and Assyrians, were strongly linked to religion.

Similarly, in the prehistoric ages that go back hundreds of thousands of years that passed over mankind, during which man was present, but history had not yet begun [to be recorded], we observe indicators of worship and ideology that were prevalent during those times. For instance, today, we see vivid and beautiful drawings of animals on the walls of remnant caves that go back tens of thousands of years. Presumably, a man in those caves at that time performed a form of worship of these drawings as his mind had not yet evolved beyond grasping only tangible or concrete aspects that he could feel or sense; hence, he would search for a deity within this circle of tangibles, and the core of his belief in God was that he believed in His existence, but this belief was still deviant.

During those times, man would suspect that God was a tangible and living being with an important role in his life, and that is why he would worship the sun at times and the moon at others, as well as the stars and different animals sometimes.

Based on all those above, it is evident that worship and religion were present even during those times, albeit in the form of myths filled with delusions, and that was due to man's limited knowledge and understanding of creation at that time.

Nonetheless, disregarding this period, we will surely fail to find any age in the [recorded] human history that is void of any ideological presence; rather, religion has always had a special standing among mankind.

Here, the reader might wonder: "You say that man cannot bear the absence of religion in his life, then why are there now in communist countries many people who don't feel this way? And how could they endure this (i.e., absence of religion)?"

In response, briefly, it is prudent to point out that the notion of genuinely irreligious individuals within materialistic, atheistic, and communist systems is wrong. These people turned away from God ﷻ and His worship and resorted to a practical form of idolatry, and they perform rituals and actions just as those who follow a religion do. For instance, communists revere and respect the statues of Lenin or the thoughts of their leaders, such as Marx and Engels, and followers of religion do the same with the shrines of prophets and divine scriptures. Hence, it is, in fact, a type of religion but in the form of worshiping idols and man: they chose religion in this image and form.

If we were to examine some religious thoughts and concepts closely, we would find that these thoughts and concepts are also present among communists who supposedly don't believe in religion. For one, we believe that it is not permissible to innovate in religion; for example, one cannot switch up prayer or Islāmic rulings or its fundamental pillars, and so it is not permitted to change or modify anything that has Islāmic reasoning and ruling into another form; this is called innovation, and it is forbidden as per Islāmic Law.

Similarly, this notion is evident among communist parties as well regarding the thoughts of Marx and Engels: it is said that Chinese communists have led a large feud against the Russian communists, with the former calling the latter "revisionists" as it appears to be a significant weakness of the Russian communists.

"You have revised the thoughts of Marx and Engels."

So, what does this imply?

Are the thoughts of Marx and Engels to be accepted without amendments, whether by addition or omission? Is revising these thoughts and innovating and modifying some fundamentals a sin or a wrong-doing?

Indeed, from the perspective of a communist, revisionism is wrong.

Therefore, what we call "innovation" is the same as what they call "revisionism" (although we analyze this topic from an academic and philosophical side and not through a political lens).

Amongst the fundamentals that comprised the divine laws was the principle stating that God's divine revelation ﷻ was infallible. Why? Because it came from God, and God ﷻ does not make mistakes. Hence, the prophets who receive divine revelation are also infallible. In this sense, communists revere communist ideals as infallible divine revelations. For instance, they say that it is fundamental to preserve the Communist Manifesto completely, that there should be no more than one party in communist nations, and that everyone born in this environment must follow this ideology. Why? Because [they believe] these principles are certain and doubt-free, people must not tire themselves in searching for a weakness in them because they are indeed free of error. Everyone in this environment must thus follow the Communist Party and its principles.

Here, a question arises: aren't Marx, Engles, Mao, Lenin, and the others merely humans like us? Isn't there a possibility that the thoughts of the present generation are superior to those of the figures above? Isn't it possible to find people with more profound and more thoughtful intellects? Why can't the ideologies of these figures be complemented, revised, corrected, and perfected? If one were to ask them [communists] these questions, they would accuse him of being a communist renegade. They label anyone who calls for revisionism a renegade and followers of religion use the same term as well, albeit with a different measure.

Hence, we notice that communists treat their leaders and theoreticians the same way we approach divine revelation, divine scriptures, and prophets and their ideas. As such, these people have established a religion for themselves, and the only difference is that they refused to take the worship of God ﷻ as a religion and instead chose to worship other people.

The Conclusion of this Part:

As this research was not based on this part, I would like to highlight what we have concluded thus far, passing through it as well:

As religion entails submitting to the truths of creation and existence, it has existed since the very first day of mankind's existence and shall remain until its very end. Moreover, man cannot bear the absence of religion in his life. He will thus always adopt a religion in some way or another, whether it is a pure and perfect religion or one void of good teachings and guidance; man can take up a religion of worshiping idols (old and new) or any other form or representation of it.

Another note that is particularly worth mentioning is that youths often ask us in their messages the following: You say that every scholar and thinker and every human surely follows a religion. And so, there is no truly materialistic person in the world. However, we see that among the philosophers in the world—even the non-communist ones—and the scholars and experts in natural sciences, many individuals don't believe in any deity. So, how can you say that religion is ever-present in man's life and shall remain so?

However, we think that many of these people believe in God and not the idol. Upon close inspection, we conclude that these people are saying: "We did not find a god when we autopsied the human body and dissected it for research purposes." Here, what is meant by "god" is the idol because if this god were to be a physical entity found inside the human body and if it could be felt using the autopsy tools and examined in the laboratory, then it is not a god; rather, it is a type of idol.

Therefore, when an individual says that he could not find God in the autopsy room and the laboratory, it means that he did not find the idol; otherwise, he must believe in God, but where? In that place, he describes it as the work of nature, and those traits that the materialists give to nature are all traits that we believe are attributed to God ﷻ. Allow me to demonstrate this with a simple example.

Why do we have two kidneys?

A scientist once wrote that one of nature's miracles is that it bestowed upon man two kidneys, although he can live with only one. Experiments have repeatedly proven that a healthy person can give his kidney to another person without the former sustaining any harm. Similarly, after both his kidneys had stopped working, the person who received a healthy kidney [by transplantation] can continue living a relatively healthy life. So, if man can live with only one kidney, why did God bestow upon him two?

In response, this same materialist scientist said that nature had considered the future and thus gave the man a spare kidney as backup, and this is similar to how a car needs one spare tire at least when it journeys in the desert so that it does not get stranded in the middle of the desert. In this sense, nature has also given man two kidneys instead of one so that he does not lose his way in the desert of life; if one of his kidneys were to stop functioning, he could still live with the other, or he could donate it to someone else and save them from death!

In this response, they noticeably give nature attributes of reason, feeling, management, and purposefulness, the ability to plan carefully for the future, and encompassing knowledge. But is anyone characterized by these traits except God ﷻ? Or can these traits be attributed to mindless elements that lack cognition and perception?

The following is another example in this regard:

Why did nature bestow upon man a bigger stomach than the magnitude of his need? Some people suffer from ulcers in their stomachs, and they undergo surgery that removes half or even a third of their stomach and then live ordinarily with what remains of their stomach. Hence, man can live with half a stomach, so why was he given this larger-than-needed stomach?

In response, they [materialists] say that "nature" thought ahead and predicted that a part of the stomach might stop functioning someday; thus, it decided to give man more than what he needed as a precaution in case the need arises.

As such, let us ponder the following: Does nature have a mind and the ability to reason to think of man's future and give him a preventive part to survive and continue his life? Can we even say about a system that has no mind or feelings, rather one that is blind and deaf and does not have a specific purpose, program, or information?

The purpose is most often attributed to those who can think and reason; for instance, we say, "I have come to this place to participate in this seminar, and you have come to find a life plan through this research."

Thus, purpose is always an element specific to beings of rationality, knowledge, and awareness. According to materialists who perceive nature as a being without feelings and that a plan, program, and calculation do not govern the cause-effect system, what is nature's purpose? What is the meaning of purpose? What is the importance of planning for the future? What is the meaning of a plan?

As such, it is evident that nature has a different meaning; what they call nature is the same as what we call God, and all these attributes—knowledge, power, wisdom, the capacity for planning, and purpose—belong to God ﷻ.

Every Scholar has a Religious Ideology

Some may prefer to avoid hearing about this topic from us and would only listen to the accounts of Western scholars and their testimonies and confessions regarding these issues. Hence, we refer to the following excerpt from the sayings of the famous scholar Einstein, one of the most renowned thinkers of our era, to clarify how every scholar has a religious ideology. Even the most established scientists admit that every scholar, scientist, and thinker in the world has a kind of fixed religious ideology, and even those who are seemingly the forerunners in the ranks of atheists and materialists and those who deny God ﷻ are not without ideology. Religion and ideology are inevitable human needs that cannot be overlooked, even if some try to appear otherwise, and they are life necessities that cannot be escaped, even if some try to ignore them.

Einstein goes even further with this above notion and says:

Over all those long centuries and ages, scientists, thinkers, explorers, and innovators have made scientific progress owing to a main driver: their religious ideology. If it weren't for this ideology, they would not have been able to make these discoveries. This could seem strange to some, but it is clear to us that all scientists used to draw the inspiration strength—in fact—needed to make their scientific discoveries from their belief in God.

Let us examine closely the following extract from Einstein's book *The World As I See It*, which was translated and published in many languages:

You will hardly find an intellectual person with no religious feelings. But it is different from the religion of the naive man. For the latter, God is a being whose care one hopes to benefit and whose punishment one fears - a sublimation of a feeling similar to that of a child for its father. As for the scientist who believes in universal causality, what religion does he believe in? His religion takes the form of a precise natural law that is invigorating and reveals, at times, an intelligence and mysteries of such superiority that, compared with it, all the systematic thinking and acting of human beings is an utterly insignificant reflection.

Religion for a scientist differs from that of a regular person; most people get close to God out of fear of Him or yearning for heaven, but the scientist's religiosity stems from the workings of existence and the laws of creation. So, when he [the scientist] observes this miraculous and confusing system, he is overcome with confusion and admiration combined with a refreshing feeling, pushing him to explore the laws that govern this world. As he slowly uncovers the laws and systems of this world, all the effort he had invested and all the troubles he had endured on the journey seem primarily insignificant in the face of this law he discovered. Thus, a sense of tranquility fills his soul, erasing the pain and fatigue of the journey.

While reading Einstein's thoughts, I remembered a saying by Imām ʿAlī b. Abī Ṭālib ﷺ:

> "O' my Lord, I did not worship you for fear of your punishment [Hell] nor longing for your reward [Heaven]; but rather, I found

You worthy of being worshiped, so I worshiped You...".

"Every being shall return to You, and this miraculous system is Your creation, and it is for this system and this existence and for You, Your knowledge, and Your Wisdom that are endless and inescapable; it is for all this that I worship You."

In this sense, after around 1400 years on the Imām's saying, Einstein came to say that the religion of a thinker is built on this miraculous and confusing natural law of the world of creation around which his thoughts revolve. Most of his achievements take the form of deciphering some parts of this enormous world and revealing the intricacies of some of its mysteries.

All of the above clarify a few fundamental matters:

1. It has become clear that religion is, in principle, submitting to the truths of existence and creation in the face of God ﷻ and His rulings. Moreover, all the religions and divine laws complement each other, on the one hand, and are integral to man's instincts, body, and soul.

2. Religion has been present over the different ages of mankind because man is in a sturdy and inevitable relationship with the mortal world and can only submit to the truths of existence whether he likes it or not. As such, religion is deeply rooted in man's being and shall remain so, but only its forms and representations may differ.

3. Those who, at present, claim that they do not have a religion are, in reality, nonetheless committed to religion in the form of worshiping humans, or they have used a different name ("nature") for what we call God, giving this nature they believe all the attributes of God ﷻ.

Overall, this is the summation of all the issues that must be considered on the path to understanding the true meaning of religion. Now, onto the next step; let us investigate what benefits we reap from this religion that we have defined in the above three points.

The Hopeful Future

In the conclusion of this research, it is prudent to recall this vital point: Contrary to what those who have lost hope think that the pillars of religion in the circle of human society have decayed and weakened, I believe in the complete opposite; I see that man today is leaning towards religion, particularly Islām, and that mankind has started to approach the beliefs and thoughts of the prophets. This is not merely heresy; I have seen the truth through the many experiences I've had mingling and corresponding with people of various backgrounds. This means that I do say what I do based on a scholarly book I read; rather, I base my argument on my personal experiences.

Hence, we must be optimistic regarding the future. Indeed, the end of the current society will be better than the past because the faith of the youth has strengthened, and the pillars of religion have taken a sturdier and deeper root.

Don't worry about the corruption that has surfaced in society nowadays; if the means of corruption available today were present two hundred years ago, society would be much worse than today. The only reason corruption was less widespread then was the absence of the means we have today. Nonetheless, this corruption has exhausted people and led to feelings of failure, confusion, and desperation; hence, reform is of utmost necessity.

Today, we observe various religious centers and committees for youths in this country. Perhaps the founders never imagined that such a tremendous gathering of students, teachers, professors, scholars, and people from different backgrounds would ever occur—in some cases, even meetings to study Islām are held over the summer, during which most people seek to relax and have fun.

Therefore, let us be optimistic, for we aren't alone in this journey, and the future of religion is much better off than its past. The bonds of faith will surely strengthen, and the following will clarify how mankind has started growing closer to God ﷻ through science and knowledge. By following in the footsteps of the prophets, we are stepping forward in assuredness, confidence, and cognizance, each one of us becoming a messenger in our surroundings, whether it is the school, university, workplace, or any other place, and a bright guiding light for others.

Benefits and Consequences

As we previously stated, this research aims to investigate what ramifications and impacts religion has imprinted in man's life and what achievements it has realized for mankind. Accordingly, in the first part, we shed light on the true meaning of religion from a philosophical point of view and the side of reason and Islāmic logic. The second part, on the other hand, revolves around the benefits and impacts of religion in people's lives. This is a rather broad topic because religion influences all the life affairs of man, and it has always harbored a close connection to people's lives throughout history. To discuss the influence and impact of religion on mankind extensively and comprehensively, it is prudent to include the following points:

1. The psychological impact of religion

2. The role of religion in establishing and achieving social justice

3. The role of religion in fighting corruption

4. The political and economic impacts of religion

In light of the above, it is evident that the consequences and impacts of religion on people's lives are multi-dimensional, and each dimension requires independent research.

In this short research, we explore only one side of this topic: the role of religion in reviving intellect and reason. In other words, how can religion give rise to an intellectual transformation within the circle of society? In this regard, we shall address only one part of this topic within the impacts of religion: the role and impacts of religion in the intellectual revolution and the revival of reason.

Here, the reader might wonder why we chose to explore the benefits and role of religion in this aspect over all the others. Reviving intellect and reason is of utmost importance and sensitivity, more so than the others, as most social revolutions occur under the influence of these intellectual and mental transformations. If a nation's intellect and mind were to stay at rest, then all other aspects [of life] shall always remain stunted, and their potential would never be realized.

Proof of this matter is the lives of the prophets and messengers; God's prophets and messengers sought to reform societies by reviving their mental and intellectual capacities. Through this intellectual transformation, reform began to take root in the world.

Based on the above, we speak clearly and honestly about the role and impact of religion in the revival and transformation of the intellect in human societies. Here, it is prudent to mention the following:

As we know, philosophers belong to two categories: theist philosophers who believe in the existence of God and that He is the source of knowledge and power that govern this world, and they constitute the grand majority of philosophers worldwide; and materialist philosophers, and it is possible that the individuals in this category have mixed up the naming of God, as we previously discussed, but they are now included in this direction nonetheless.

The Difference between Theist and Materialist Philosophers

How do theist and materialist philosophers differ?

In principle, some wrongly assume that the difference between theist and materialist philosophers lies in worshiping God and that theist philosophers believe in the first cause [i.e., the idea that the universe is caused by something that is itself uncaused] and the ultimate cause of all causes as opposed to materialists. In this sense, their difference would lie in their belief or disbelief in the first cause. According to some, theist philosophers believe that all living beings and creatures and the world of existence are the results of a cause that does not have a reason itself, describing it as the "necessary existence" that is self-created and does not owe its existence to any other existent being. Conversely, materialists don't believe in the first cause.

As such, some [wrongly] perceive the crux of the difference between materialism and theism to be the belief or disbelief in the first cause.

However, this is an entirely wrong perception because all philosophers, materialists, and theists believe in the first cause without exception; they all believe in an eternal being that has always been there and will remain forever. The difference is that while theists believe this concept to be "God", the materialists view that this fundamental being is "matter".

In the materialists' view, the matter is the first cause, the cause of all causes, and it is self-created: a necessary existence that is not caused by another cause, is eternal and has always been ever-present. Conversely, theists believe God to be this first cause.

Therefore, both parties perceive that this universe has a first cause, but one believes it to be "matter" while the other believes it to be "God".

In this regard, I recall a saying by the famous English philosopher Bertrand Russel, whose ideas have garnered much attention in the present day and whom I found to have fallen into the same mistake in the matter of knowing God, for he says in his book *Why I Am Not a Christian*, "I am not a Christian; rather, I am a materialist..." In a lecture published in the book above, he spoke of this in detail.

At the beginning of the book, Russel says honestly, "In my youth, I used to believe in God, and I was a true Christian; I used to believe in the existence of a creator. However, due to my scientific and intellectual progress over time, I overcame the belief that there is a cause for every existing thing, that the universe has an ultimate cause, and that

'God' is the first cause. This deductive reasoning was the basis for my belief in God. Still, after a while, my faith in God wavered and faded when confronted with the following statement: If the universe has a cause. God is this cause, and if a universal law governs all that exists, then isn't there a cause for the creator as well?

This statement left a deep imprint in my soul and mind and put a stop to my religious beliefs such that I abandoned them entirely, and I concluded that the belief in a cause for everything is wrong."

This is the same issue that the youth face today. However, commenting on Russel's thoughts above, it is prudent to highlight two points:

First, The concept of one ultimate cause for everything is not proof of knowing God. That is because materialists, too, believe in this concept, except they view matter as the leading cause; as such, they also believe in the first cause. Therefore, belief in the first cause is not related to knowing God. But the question remains: why does everyone think this universe has a self-created first cause and is not the result of another cause? The answer is simple: assuming that the universe is the result of a cause, and this cause is the result of another cause, and so on, then this requires the belief in a chain of causality. They find this implausible because it leads to an infinite series of causes that contradict the idea of everything needing to acquire its existence from an existing entity. Hence, it is prudent that there be an entity that is self-created and does not need another being because even infinite causes are the results of another cause, and endless needs need others, too. For instance, if we put the number zero next to another zero and repeat this endlessly, we would not get any number. Similarly, if we were to extend this chain of causes and effects in the universe infinitely, then it is as though we are merely adding zeros next to zeros, trying to [in vain] to obtain any number.

When this implausibility became evident, they had to halt this chain of causality at a certain point, which they then made into the crux of the existence of a self-created first cause that is not the result of any other cause. This entity must be reached and understood, and it is what we call the "necessary existence": the materialists view it as the cause of everything and an eternal being, while theists believe it is God.

Therefore, Russel fell into a logical fallacy when he said that he abandoned the principle of the first cause because whoever denies this concept is neither materialist nor theist; rather, he becomes the proponent of an endless chain of causality that cannot be resolved.

Second: When we say that every existing being needs a cause, we mean by the term "every existing being" every being that is possible [i.e., does not exist necessarily through itself; thus, its possible existence depends upon whether or not it is caused to exist] and is in need [for another] and whose existence originates outside itself. This term is authentic, as every possible being inevitably needs a cause to exist. However, it is not true for the creator or the first cause: a possible being whose existence originates outside itself needs a cause [to exist resultantly], so can this law also include the creator? The answer is no. This law does not encompass the first [uncaused] cause because every existing being is in need [for another], and every being whose existence originates outside itself (which is what is termed as "possible existence") needs a cause. As for the eternal entity—the self-originated necessary existence—does not need a cause [to exist], whether it be matter or a creator.

Examples for Clarification:

Most of you have probably heard of these well-known analogies:

It is said that everything requires light to be illuminated, so does the same apply to light itself? Does light need light as well to illuminate? Similarly, everything needs water to become moist, so does water also need water to become moist? And does the word "everything" include water as well? In the same sense, everything needs fire to become hot, so does fire also need fire to become hot? If food needs salt to become salty, does salt need salt, too, to become salty?

These general laws don't apply to these elements themselves. When we say that food needs salt to become salty, then this saltiness is not contained in the food itself; rather, it is acquired from outside the food. The same is the case for heat: it is not present within everybody and is only procured from outside this body, which needs it. As for fire itself, it does not need fire to procure heat and thus become hot.

This same concept is present in philosophy under the heading "everything that is an accident [accidental property] must end with that which exists in itself [essence]", meaning that every accidental element has a source to return to. This source does not need anything else.

That is the case for "existence". The existing beings derive their existence from someplace else because they are not immortal, and these beings have a history; the formation of the Earth and sky and the planets and solar system all have a history—it is said that our solar system is over four thousand million years old! Hence, this system has a history, and since it was not present before four thousand million years ago, its existence originates from outside itself. Thus, it is prudent to refer to an eternal first cause that is not the result of any other.

Based on all the above, we conclude that the difference between the materialists and theists is not the belief in the first cause, and it is wrong to assume that materialists deny the theists' belief that the universe has an eternal first cause. Instead, both parties believe in a self-created first cause that exists in itself.

Here, what is the actual difference between branches? Well, the difference between materialism and theism resides entirely in one point. Theist philosophers say this eternal first cause possesses knowledge and wisdom and has a purpose, plan, and program. On the other hand, materialists view matter as the first cause: it is eternal but lacks knowledge, wisdom, and purpose, and it has nothing to do with planning and systems. Instead, it is [to materialists] random accidents and causes void of feeling and wisdom that gathered together and resulted in this universe; hence, this world is the result of that matter without a foundation of reason, wisdom, a plan, or a purpose.

Therefore, the crux of the difference between both branches lies in attributing (or not) knowledge and wisdom to the eternal cause of this world, as both believe in the existence of the first cause. Still, one attributes knowledge and wisdom to it, while the other denies that.

Now, after clarifying that the difference revolves around "knowledge" and "ignorance" regarding the ultimate cause of existence, let us look back on this broad universal system of the world of creation and existence. Upon examining the existing beings in this universe, can we find a trace of knowledge and wisdom that can be attributed to this [first] cause, or perhaps not? Let us examine this universal system to determine which of the two branches [theism or materialism] is correct.

Both believe in the first cause, but they differ in whether or not this cause has wisdom and knowledge. Here, it is prudent to say, as previously indicated, that materialists unconsciously believe in the existence of a universal system in this world. Thus, owing to this belief, they believe in the principle of reason and wisdom in this world, although they would not admit it.

Simple Example:

Medical sciences have witnessed discoveries and a new horizon in recent years. For the first time in the history of medicine and surgery, Dr. Barnard was able to perform a heart transplant; he extracted another [recently deceased] human's heart and transplanted it into the chest of another person whose heart had stopped working, bringing him to the edge of death. Still, Dr. Barnard could keep the patient alive for approximately five hundred days. Although Mr. Blaiberg did die as a result of his body's resistance against foreign bodies, he was still able to live with the transplanted heart for five hundred days.

A question arises: Did Dr. Barnard make this miraculous and wonderful medical achievement based only on his knowledge and intellectual ability? The average person would retort that it is Dr. Barnard's own doing. However, a more discerning person would say that mankind—in its entirety—contributed to this achievement; this doctor had studied at some university, and he had professors who had benefited from others' ideas and the resources and experiences accumulated over thousands of years. Throughout the history of medicine, these ideas and notions formed gradually and were written down in books studied in universities. In this way, Dr. Barnard studied these past sciences and reached this outcome [heart transplant] by benefiting from the experiences accumulated over thousands of years.

Therefore, Dr. Barnard dotted the end of the line after his scientist ancestors had prepared the crux and paved the way for the caravan of knowledge and human intellect to advance.

In conclusion, ultimately, for the heart transplant operation to succeed, it needed a rich exchange of ideas and accumulated efforts of scientists over a few thousand years!

Is this achievement possible without knowledge and wisdom? Certainly not. Without the collective efforts and expertise of scholars and genius minds over thousands of years, this operation could not have been achieved, and it would not have been possible to transfer a heart from one person to another.

Here, a question arises: if I want to replace a light bulb, would this process—which would, in some cases, require precision and technical skill—require more knowledge and wisdom than manufacturing this same light bulb? Is the act of replacing the light bulb more important than the process of manufacturing it?!

The heart transplant operation is considered a miraculous procedure in the field of medicine. Despite its great significance, it is ultimately the same as the act of replacing a light bulb. Thus, this procedure is useless in the face of the heart and the cardiovascular system: its intricacies, mysteries, precise parts, and astonishing mechanisms.

In our present world, no scientist would dare to say that the heart transplant operation is made possible due to the collective efforts of scientific minds over thousands of years while claiming that the cardiovascular system owes its existence to nature. This nature has no mind or feeling at all. Physically speaking, nature does not even have the cognition of a one-day-old newborn, so how can it create a heart?

The Importance of the Heart

On this note, we must explore another matter to reach the all-important overarching outcome of this research.

A while ago, I read in a newspaper that experts prepared an artificial heart and planted it in the chest of a patient bedridden in a hospital. This person could not move, or the artificial heart would stop working. The heart functioned for around six days, costing about 30 million Toman! So, it cost them about five million Tomans per day to keep this person alive. All these costs, intellect, and scientific progress in different fields finally enabled them to install an artificial heart. An expert commented, "I did not know I was *this* rich. If the cost of a heart per day is five million Toman, how wealthy would I be if I lived for fifty years? How rich am I if that is the value of this single body part?"

What this implies is as follows: Does this astonishing system that we live in hinge on our existence or our hearts, brains, or eyes only? A Russian scientist once described the intricacies of the human eye, "The most beautiful and intricate structure to be seen in our world today is that of the human eye." So, the first cause of this universe is a lack of knowledge, awareness, and wisdom. If so, how did it conceive this universe in that state [of ignorance]?

Indeed, this is unimaginable, and as previously indicated, materialists themselves unconsciously believe in this system and thus also believe in the existence of the principle of knowledge and wisdom in this system, even if they do not admit it or notice it.

To conclude this matter, let's consider the following points:

1. Materialists and theists do not differ in believing in a first cause and an immortal entity.

2. They only differ on whether or not this first cause has the attributes of knowledge and wisdom.

3. The overall view of the world of existence predicates that the workings of this universe are based on a sense of knowledge, wisdom, and organization.

With all that established, we shall move forward to the outcome and examine the role of religious faith and belief in reviving and developing the human intellect. Our intellect stems from this faith and trust in God and religion.

Some of Einstein's Thoughts

Here, I shall cite some of what Einstein has said in this regard, highlighting a beautiful expression I wish you to read closely.

On page 59 of his book *The World As I See It*, Einstein says, "I believe that existentialism is the most significant driver of scientific research. Under existentialism, it is prudent to conduct research in all branches of natural sciences [that is due to his belief that existentialism is the right philosophical belief, and this belief system assumes the existence of the principle of knowledge and wisdom]. Those who are aware of the true meaning behind the unimaginable efforts of scientists and thinkers and, more importantly, the sacrifices and efforts of the scientific community in explaining and interpreting the scientists' theories know the tremendous energy behind these reactions that are the basis for all these astonishing innovations and responsible for unveiling the truth of the laws of life."

Then he concludes, "It is such commitment to or belief in a universal system of existence and this curiosity that gave Newton the ability and power to endure the pain of loneliness and silence for many years so that he can explore and clarify the force of universal gravitation and the astronomical system." Strange. He is saying that when Newton first saw the apple fall from the tree to the ground, he contemplated it for a few years. What prompted him to think of this when he could have concluded that the apple falling from the tree resulted from coincidence and randomness?

However, somewhere deep within his mind, Newton knew that gravity works according to a specific law and system and that the whole universe is governed by a system, which is the result of a wise and knowing cause or principle. Inevitably, this led Newton to years of research and investigation until he was able to discover and define the law of gravity as "that every particle attracts every other particle in the universe with a force that is proportional to the product of their masses and inversely proportional to the square of the distance between their centers." Had Newton been a real materialist, believing that the universe is the result of a cause without knowledge or wisdom, then he would have surely abandoned this scope of the search for a system and a law, as it would've been plausible for him that randomness can generate such a state of gravitation. Therefore, it is clear that the belief in a system [that governs the universe] was ever-present in Newton's mind.

That is also the case for Kepler, who conducted much research to discover the laws of planetary motions within the solar system. He believed in a universal system that governed and managed this planetary motion, or else he would have needed more effort and research to discover these laws over those long years.

Hence, those scientists' endless efforts reveal their belief in a universal and comprehensive system that governs this universe. Those who hold this belief must also inevitably believe that the essence of this universe is characterized by knowledge and wisdom.

Einstein continues to say that this personal religious feeling enabled them [scientists] to sacrifice and endure many hardships and failures over the centuries.

Furthermore, Einstein quotes a contemporary saying that is of utmost importance to university students, particularly those involved in the different branches of natural sciences, "Those who possess a deep sense of religion and mystery in the era of matter are the only ones who truly and seriously contribute to sciences!" He means to refer to those who believe in this universal system and seek to uncover its secrets and mysteries, and if there weren't a belief in such a system, then no real efforts would've been made.

In this sense, if Maeterlinck had not harbored the belief that a system governed the life of ants, he would not have spent 20 years researching it. His ardent belief in the existence of a plan and a purpose in the life of ants pushed him to explore it and write it down in his book. Hence, anyone who believes in a system that governs the world of existence must also, as a result, believe that the cause of this existence possesses knowledge and wisdom because it would be impossible to unveil this system without knowledge and understanding.

In this sense, we find that the primary impact of religion and the belief in God on man is that it pushes him to contemplate the intricacies of the universe, making him such an avid explorer of the world. Man thus seeks to prove that the minor happenings of this world can have a solid and resonating effect because they are the result of a principle that is endlessly wise and knowledgeable, in addition to being the product of this principle's power. This system is not ordinary, and it is thus prudent to closely and precisely examine and contemplate its parts.

On the other hand, if a man believed that this system results from a nature that lacks knowledge and wisdom, then there is no reason or justification for contemplating and investigating the minor parts of this universe and employing intellectual and mental abilities.

Ultimately, the foremost impact of faith and belief in God on mankind is the revival of the intellect and mind.

In this regard, I want to highlight another important outcome of this research, particularly as it pertains to the educated youth today: Looking at the exemplary approach of Prophet

Muḥammad ﷺ, we find that he, too, invited people to contemplation and reflection under this religion and belief in God ﷻ, as the Maker ﷻ says in the Noble Qur'ān:

﴿إِنَّ فِي خَلْقِ ٱلسَّمَٰوَٰتِ وَٱلْأَرْضِ وَٱخْتِلَٰفِ ٱلَّيْلِ وَٱلنَّهَارِ لَأَيَٰتٍ لِّأُوْلِي ٱلْأَلْبَٰبِ﴾

﴿*'inna fī khalqi s-samāwāti wa-l-'arḍi wa-khtilāfi l-layli wa-n-nahāri la-'āyātin li-'ulī l-albāb*﴾

﴿ٱلَّذِينَ يَذْكُرُونَ ٱللَّهَ قِيَٰمًا وَقُعُودًا وَعَلَىٰ جُنُوبِهِمْ وَيَتَفَكَّرُونَ فِي خَلْقِ ٱلسَّمَٰوَٰتِ وَٱلْأَرْضِ﴾

﴿*ᵃlladhīna yadhkurūna llāha qiyāman wa-quʿūdan wa-ʿalā junūbihim wa-yatafakkarūna fī khalqi s-samāwāti wa-l-'arḍi*﴾

﴿*Indeed in the creation of the heavens and the earth and the alternation of night and day, there are signs for those who possess intellect. Those who remember God standing, sitting, and lying on their sides, and reflect on the creation of the heavens and the earth*﴾[16]

---

[16] Sūrat Āl ʿImrān, Verses 190-191.

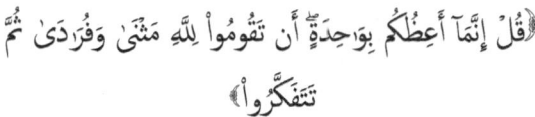

*qul 'innamā 'a'iẓukum bi-wāḥidatin 'an taqūmū
li-llāhi mathnā wa-furādā thumma tatafakkarū*

*Say, 'I give you just a single advice: that you rise up
for God's sake, in pairs or singly, and then reflect*[17]

The act of reflection received such great
importance that it became one of Islām's greatest
and best acts of worship, according to narrations
from the Prophet and Imām 'Alī b. Abī Ṭālib in the
notable books of Hadith:

> "The best of worship is the continuous
> contemplation of God and His power."[18]

> "There is no worship like contemplating
> the creation of God ﷻ."[19]

---

[17] Sūrat Saba, Verse 46.

[18] Rayshahrī, Āyatullāh Muḥammad, *Mīzān al-Ḥikmah*,
Vol. 7, p. 543.

[19] Ibid.

The Benefits of the Religious Movement

Someone might wonder: what did the Muslims achieve through the revival of their intellectual and mental powers under the influence of their belief in God and the true religion?

In response, they established the foundations of a pristine civilization and achieved spectacular progress that directed the world's attention toward the Islāmic dynasties for centuries.

Today's youth must realize the importance of reading, particularly regarding the scientific renaissance in the early days of Islām (i.e., from the second to fifth century), including the books that foreigners authored about Islām. The youth needs to realize the scientific progress and transformation that Islām has produced in the many branches of science. This is ultimately what faith, belief in God, religion, and contemplation have provided mankind with.

I always recommend books for the youth to read and dedicate their time to—as their readings should not only be confined to their school or university books but also benefit from other various books. Among these books is *Mīrāth al-*

Islām. This book provides an account of the elements that the Europeans took or derived from the Muslims and Eastern nations in their scientific renaissance. Thirteen professors from London universities authored this book, and within it, English orientalists explain the contributions that Muslims and Islāmic scholars have made to the sciences and knowledge. I shall report to you two topics from this book, as evidenced in the following.

Who is Jābir b. Ḥayyān?

Jābir b. Ḥayyān is one of the Islāmic scholars who have become famous in the West and among Westerners, and he is known as the founder of the science of chemistry. The chemistry as we know it today was taken from the books of Jābir b. Ḥayyān in the early days.

Jābir b. Ḥayyān was raised among Muslims and under Islāmic leadership, with Imām Jaʿfar al-Ṣādiq at the helm.

Let us take a look at what Westerners say about Jābir b. Ḥayyān.

Dr. Meyerhof, among the greatest professors of London universities, wrote the following about him: "Jābir b. Ḥayyān was known around the world as the founder of chemistry among the Arabs, and there are now around a hundred books in chemistry authored by Jābir b. Ḥayyān. The impact that Jābir b. Ḥayyān left behind throughout the history of chemistry in Europe are prominent. This man conducted many experiments and posited many theories and hypotheses relating to chemistry. To better know and understand Jābir b. Ḥayyān, it is prudent to read his many chemistry books, some of which were copied into Latin. These books, which became his legacy, include many important and complex matters that still mystify scientists today, and he posed many problems in his books that scientists cannot solve even to this day." Meyerhof continues to mention many such matters about Jābir ibn Ḥayyān, but to keep this brief, we shall not add them here.

Unfortunately, the books of Jābir b. Ḥayyān in Arabic are not available. However, their Latin translations are readily present in libraries across Europe!

It is said that the number of books found to be authored by this Islāmic scholar reaches a hundred books in different branches of chemistry.

If we were to wonder about the secrets and factors that drove this scientific renaissance, we would find out that it goes back to the progress that the then-backward nations achieved under the influence of religion. Why not admit the truth? As Iranians, how many scholars or scientists did we have before Islām took root in our country? How many scholars like Bourzerjomaher are there in the ancient history of Iran?

On the other hand, the religious renaissance gave rise to many scholars and scientists such as Ibn Sīna, Zakariyya al-Rāzī, Nassir al-Dīn al-Tūsī, and the like. All these great scholars appeared after Islām spread in the region. So why would we avoid the truth that the history of our country before Islām saw a much too small number of scholars?

This merit is what Islām achieved for mankind in its entirety and for us Iranians, in particular in the context of knowledge and intellect, in addition to reviving long-dead notions. We undoubtedly possess tremendous will and extensive capabilities, but they still require guidance and instruction to flourish.

Introduction to Ibn al-Haytham

Ibn al-Haytham was a prominent Muslim physicist and genius, one of the scholars of the fourteenth-century AH. He lived around eighty years, from 350 AH to 430 AH. Nicknamed "Abū ʿAlī", Ibn al-Haytham is originally from Baṣrah, ʿIrāq, and authored many influential books. Europeans Latinized his name as Alhazen. According to Meyerhof, he invested substantial efforts in the research on light.

Ibn al-Haytham left for Cairo during the ʿAbbāsid Caliphate, and there, he sought to find a solution to the issue of regulating the Nile's rising water and flooding. However, he could not accomplish this task, eliciting the anger of the ʿAbbāsid Caliph at that time, known as al-Ḥakīm bi-Amr Allāh. Consequently, he was forced to stay hidden until the Caliph died, and during that period, he spent his time writing and researching in the fields of medicine, physics, and mathematics.

The crux of his writings was his research on light; although the original copy he wrote in Arabic was lost, its Latin translation is still available. Ibn al-Haytham discussed and built up Euclid's theory on the eye. He wrote about many important subjects regarding colors, the propagation and refraction of light, and the necessary experiments to determine the angle of light refraction and reflection. Moreover, to this day, his theory is known among Europeans as Alhazen's theory.

Ibn Sīna and His Books

European orientalists admit that Ibn Sīna's book *The Canon of Medicine*—considered one of our books on medicine—has been translated and printed sixteen times in Europe during the last thirty years of the fifteenth century only. The book was reprinted around twenty times in the sixteenth century, meaning that this book was reissued in Europe around thirty-six times in a relatively short period. For centuries, this book was studied in European medical schools, and doctors used to draw inspiration from it and refer to it in their medical practices.

This is just a glimpse into the great knowledge and wisdom Muslims demonstrated. So, where did all this flourishment come from? Indeed, it came to be after the intellectual renaissance and the revival of the intellect and mind in the Islāmic World under the influence of faith in religion and belief in God. The Muslims themselves made all these discoveries in the sciences and achieved this spectacular progress.

The Importance of the Mosque

It is important to note that, according to historical accounts, all teaching and learning at that time used to occur at the mosques. The mosque, known as a place for the elderly, used to be a center of knowledge and culture—a university, even.

Even if studies in the field of medicine were confined to hospitals, all other sciences and subject matter were taught at mosques. This means that Muslims led this global scientific renaissance from these same mosques. Despite this, some people still come to us Muslims and describe us as backward people.

So we wonder, is it this Islām that you describe as backward?

It is the Muslim who adhered to the Islāmic teachings, utilized his intellect, and turned the mosque into a university and his home into a center of intellect, upholding his values in all aspects of life, and it is his Muslim scholars who played prominent roles in various fields. Are we that Muslim [of that time when Muslims flourished]? Did we find ourselves lagging back due to that [upholding the true teachings of Islām and intellect]? No. Instead, Islām's rulings were stalled, and its programs and teachings needed to be addressed and remembered. Nothing remains of Islām except the appearance and formalities, which have ultimately set us back...

Bayt al-Maqdis in the Islāmic History

Here, I find it necessary to highlight a cause of utmost importance, one that causes me great pain every time I think of it, with God as my witness.

Every time I take a glimpse at the history of the Crusades, I notice that Muslims—as Gustave Le Bon says—were always in an impenetrable position in terms of politics and military. And it is no simple matter for the whole of Europe and the Christian world to move all at once and put aside all their differences to wage war for years just so that they can take control of Bayt al-Maqdis (al-Masjid al-Aqṣā). History recorded that they were at war for two hundred years, for generations successively, leaving behind millions of casualties and injuries and losing millions in money. However, they could not snatch Bayt al-Maqdis from the Muslims even after two hundred years, when Salaḥuddīn al-Ayyūbi [Saladin] raised the fluttering banner of Islām on Bayt al-Maqdis, reasserting the Muslim's authority on it.

Are we, who wasted this legacy of two hundred years in a mere six days, the same Muslims as the Muslims of those past times? They were Muslims, and so were we! So, what happened?

And still, despite all that, we wonder why we, Muslims, were set back and lagged behind everyone else. How could we not, when the Muslims today are so divided, ignorant, and purposeless, only touching upon the formalities of Islām; they are even unaware of the history of Islām—to the extent that it is a non-Muslim who wrote a book on the Prophet Muḥammad ﷺ, sending it to them from Europe. It is titled *Muḥammad, A Prophet Who Must Be Known Again*.

Ultimately, Muslims are lagging far behind other nations now because they have distanced themselves from Islām. As such, unfortunately, al-Masjid al-Aqṣā, which was the Muslims' first

Qiblah [the direction to which they pray], has now fallen into the hands of the enemies who long to burn it down.

Truthfully, this is a disgrace of the highest level for the Muslims. They used to stand in the direction of the al-Masjid al-Aqṣā and pray; it was their first Qiblah. It is the most holy place of sanctity in Islām, second to the Kaʿbah and al-Masjid al-Ḥarām in Makkah. How did the Muslims descend into such a state that their first Qiblah fell into the hands of their enemies? The famous historian Arnold Toynbee—a foreigner—describes these enemies as follows: "No one can exonerate those who occupied the Islāmic lands because the fire happened during their occupation while they were guarding the so-called '[site of] protection'!"

So why didn't the Muslims themselves protect their holy places?

On this note, it is prudent that we, the Muslim nation, wake up. The way to victory and happiness is only paved by reviving the intellect and realizing the necessities of this age and the global situation, benefiting from the diverse energies of people and referring back to our spectacular history as a backbone.

God ﷻ says in the Noble Qur'ān,

﴿إِنَّمَا يَعْمُرُ مَسَاجِدَ ٱللَّهِ مَنْ ءَامَنَ بِٱللَّهِ وَٱلْيَوْمِ ٱلْآخِرِ وَأَقَامَ
ٱلصَّلَوٰةَ وَءَاتَى ٱلزَّكَوٰةَ وَلَمْ يَخْشَ إِلَّا ٱللَّهَ فَعَسَىٰ أُوْلَٰٓئِكَ أَن يَكُونُوا۟
مِنَ ٱلْمُهْتَدِينَ﴾

﴿'innamā ya'muru masājida llāhi man 'āmana bi-
llāhi wa-l-yawmi l-'ākhiri wa-'aqāma ṣ-ṣalāta wa-
'ātā z-zakāta wa-lam yakhsha 'illā llāha fa-'asā
'ulā'ika 'an yakūnū mina l-muhtadīnᵃ﴾

﴿*Only those shall maintain God's mosques who*
believe in God and the Last Day, and maintain the
prayer, and give the zakat, and fear no one except
God. They, hopefully, will be among the guided﴾[20]

Building and maintaining mosques and centers of
monotheism and greatness is easy for those with
the following characteristics: faith in God and the
Day of Judgement, adherence to prayer, giving
alms, and fearing none but God!

The Importance of Islāmic Centers for Youths

---

[20] Sūrat al-Tawbah, Verse 18.

98

I feel greatly delighted when I enter such centers for youths because I see their adherence to the Islāmic truths in their bright faces, active bodies, and enlightened minds.

In reality, it would be most ideal if more of these centers were established—which has no doubt started to happen and must be completed—all over the country if we could enlighten the youth through them, and if more and more of such centers were built across all the Islāmic World— similar to how the Muslims were back in the day, as we had previously discussed.

We must stop wasting what we inherited from our ancestors and become righteous progeny for them so their curses don't rain down upon us. We must not let our future generations say that we were not worthy of preserving the legacy of Islām and that we lacked the competence, decency, and intellect and were thus untrustworthy!...

Academic Trips

One day, we were on a trip to visit some industrial establishments in Isfahan with a group of young men who were members of an Islāmic center. The engineers there welcomed us warmly, and I spoke for two or three minutes, saying, "Gentlemen, young men. You must commit to your studies and academic achievements and become engineers, doctors, and specialists so your country doesn't need to recruit foreign experts. Stand on your feet and rely on yourselves and your intellect, knowledge, and bright minds..."

I was glad to know that this particular institution did not have any foreign engineer, and I hope our local and official institutions follow in their lead as well!

Congregational Prayer in the Sports Field

One night, I was visiting a youth center and saw the incredible scene of a congregational prayer being held under the volleyball net. A most beautiful sight indeed!

Just as physical exercise and sports are necessary to strengthen and nurture the body—we thus find Islām to encourage it as well—prayer is another necessity to mold and discipline the soul, elevate it, and revive man's intellectual and mental capacities.

Whoever said that Islām stands in the way of sports? Among the rights of our children in Islām is to teach them beneficial sports such as marksmanship, swimming, and equestrian sports.

In closing, in such a time that we have distanced ourselves so far away from Islām, we wonder why we, as Muslims, are lagging as if we are blaming Islām [when the blame falls on us]!...

Praise be to God, the Beneficent, the Merciful